Creative Keyboard Presents

Great Literature for Piano

BAROQUE – CLASSICAL – ROMANTIC

BOOK VI
VERY DIFFICULT

Researched and Compiled by
GAIL SMITH

Visit us on the Web at http://www.melbay.com — E-mail us at email@melbay.com

Foreword

In early 19th-century Germany, the purchase of a piano commanded the interest of the new owner's entire community. The German family that ordered the piano first made a down-payment in cash. Upon completion of the piano, they paid for the balance in corn, wheat, potatoes, poultry, and firewood.

On the day that the piano was to be delivered to the new owner, the town held a festival. A band of musicians headed the procession, followed by the proud piano maker, who was borne on the shoulders of his assistants. Flowers and wreaths decorated the horse-drawn wagon which held the precious piano. Musicians, schoolmasters, and dignitaries marched in the rear.

At last the piano arrived at its destination. The delighted new owners greeted the procession warmly. The local clergyman said a prayer, blessing the new instrument as well as its craftsmen. The mayor delivered an address; the schoolmaster, doctor, and other dignitaries gave speeches. Finally, the men's chorus sang. When the piano was properly installed in its new home, everyone enjoyed a banquet and danced in celebration of this happy occasion.

In contrast, today the purchase of a piano seems no longer to be a cause for festivity and joy. Unfortunately, our generation takes such purchases for granted. We have forgotten what a treasure and gift a piano can be. We have also forgotten what a treasure and gift the great composers have given us through their beautiful musical compositions for the piano.

This new piano literature series rediscovers the "rare jewels" of piano literature. After years of research and meticulous assessment of the composers of Baroque, Classical, and Romantic music, this exciting "quest for the best" has led to a new series of eight graded books . . . all containing original compositions by the masters.

The series begins with the most easily mastered compositions, progressing to the more advanced and musically difficult selections. Pianists on all levels will enjoy this challenging, thorough, and diversified collection of piano music. In addition, an interesting biographical sketch of each composer will make these selections more meaningful to the student.

Just as flowers and wreaths decorated the horse-drawn wagon that delivered the new piano to the fortunate German villager, likewise flowers and wreaths decorate each book in this series. They serve as a reminder for us all to treasure each selection we learn and to be thankful for our magnificent musical heritage.

Gail Smith

Note to Teachers

The pieces selected in each book are in approximate order of difficulty. They are not necessarily in chronological order. Before the selections of each new composer, there is a short biographical sketch of that composer. In addition, many include a pictorial representation, as well.

Contents
Book Six

Johann Sebastian Bach
(March 21, 1685 – July 28, 1750)

The great Johann Sebastian Bach was born in German Eisenach. His brother became his teacher when his parents died when he was 10. Though so young, he longed each day for songs more difficult to play. These songs his brother did forbid and from Johann his music hid! But through the cupboard's latticed door Bach reached the tempting music score. And every moonlit night he wrote the precious copy note by note. Very secretly he learned and played, and then his brother was quite dismayed! But master of the fugue became, which won for him immortal fame. And though at last he lost his sight, his faith in God made darkness light.

Concerto in the Italian Style

Johann Sebastian Bach

11

II

15

III

Presto giojoso

24

26

Ludwig van Beethoven
(December 1770 – 1827)

Beethoven deserves to be called the Shakespeare of music. He reached the heights and depths of human emotion as no other composer has done. Beethoven's ability to imagine melodies and harmonies, composing even when he became deaf, underscores his genius.

Moonlight Sonata
(Op. 27, No. 2)

L. van Beethoven

I. **Adagio sostenuto** (♩ = 52)
sempre pp e con sordini

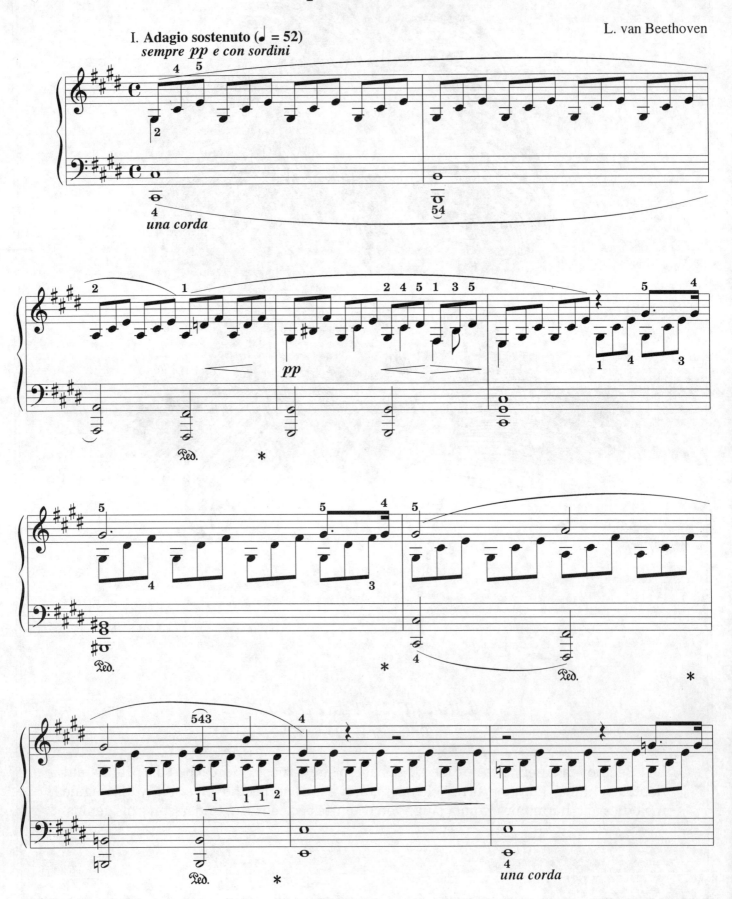

Sonata in F minor
(Op. 2, No. 1)

To Joseph Haydn

L. van Beethoven

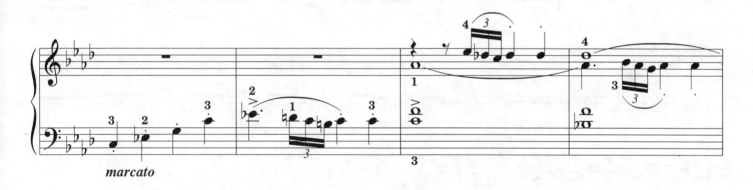

40

Johannes Brahms
(May 7, 1833 - April 3, 1897)

Brahms was a confirmed bachelor, very simple and down to earth. When he later became rich and famous, he remained a lodger in furnished rooms. Probably there was never a career less eventful than his. Brahms arose every day at five a.m., then brewed his early morning coffee himself because nobody else made it strong enough for his taste.

It is interesting to note that Brahms became a good friend of Robert Schumann, who used his influence to help Brahms get his first songs published .... which just happened to be piano pieces he had composed for the children of Robert and Clara Schumann.

Variations on a Theme by Handel

Johannes Brahms

Var. 1

44

Var. 4

Var. 5

47

Var. 6

Var. 7

Var. 8

Var. 9

poco sostenuto

Var. 12

Var. 13

Largamente, ma non più

54

Var. 14

Var. 15

Var. 16

Var. 17

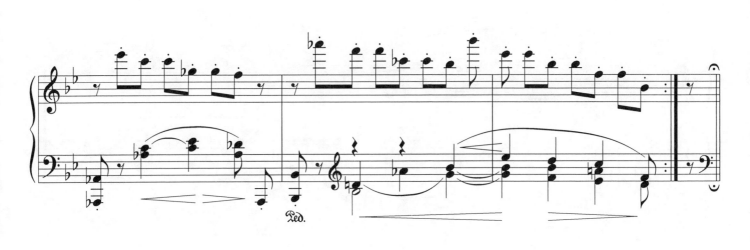

Var. 19

Var. 20

Wolfgang Amadeus Mozart
(January 27, 1756 – December 5, 1791)

Mozart and his older sister showed amazing musical talent at a very young age. Their father, Leopold, decided to commercialize their gifts and set up concert tours in many cities, including Munich, Vienna, Paris, and London. The concerts were very successful, and the children often played for royalty. Mozart began composing at age five and continued writing beautiful music all his life.

Fantasia in D minor

Wolfgang Amadeus Mozart

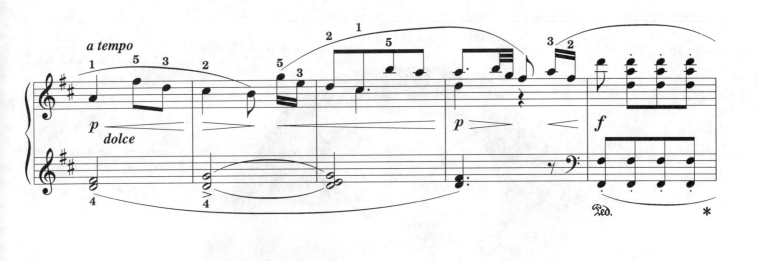

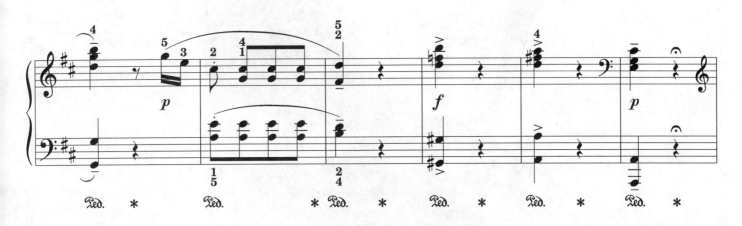

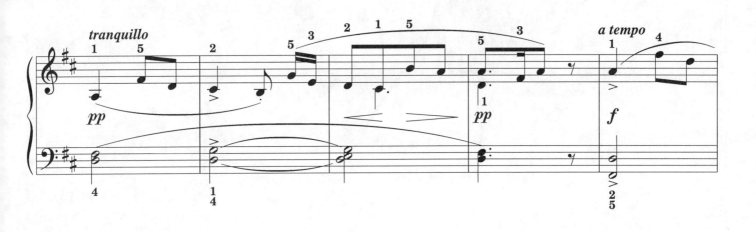

Jakob Ludwig Felix Mendelssohn
(November 3, 1809 - November 4, 1847)

Mendelssohn's father was a rich banker. All distinguished musical people who passed through Berlin visited their home. On Sunday there was always an afternoon concert by Felix and his talented sister Fanny. Mendelssohn began to compose at the age of 10. He not only composed and performed his own works, but revived the works of Johann Sebastian Bach, which had been forgotten for a hundred years.

Scherzo in E minor

Felix Mendelssohn

Allegro vivace

75

79

Frederic Francois Chopin
(February 22, 1809 – October 17, 1849)

Chopin is the only one of the world's great composers who made a specialty of the solo piano. Of his 169 works, all are exclusively for the piano. No other composer was so influential in developing modern piano technique and style. Chopin taught many piano students. Chopin wrote home, "I have to give five lessons every morning." It is not generally known that Chopin at one time intended to write a piano method. The work was never completed, but a fragment of it remains. This fragment was preserved and given by his sister to the Princess Czartoryska after his death. Here is a translation of the fragment that remains:

"No one notices inequality in the power of the notes of a scale when it is played very fast and equally, as regards time. In a good mechanism the aim is not to play everything with an equal sound, but to acquire a beautiful quality of touch and a perfect shading. For a long time players have acted against nature in seeking to give equal power to each finger. On the contrary, each finger should have an appropriate part assigned it. The thumb has the greatest power, being the thickest finger and the freest. Then comes the little finger, at the other extremity of the hand. The middle finger is the main support of the hand and is assisted by the first. Finally comes the third, the weakest one. As to this Siamese twin of the middle finger, some players try to force it with all their might to become independent. A thing impossible, and most likely unnecessary. There are, then, many different qualities of sound, just as there are several fingers. The point is to utilize the differences; and this, in other words, is the art of fingering."

Waltz in D-flat
(Op. 70, No. 3)

Frédéric Chopin

83

84

Valse
(Posthumous)

Frédéric Chopin

Trois Ecossaises

Frédéric Chopin
Op. 72, No. 3

Polonaise
(Op. 40, No. 1)

Frédéric Chopin

Revolutionary Etude
(Op. 10, No. 12)

Frédéric Chopin

Allegro con fuoco (♩ = 160)

105

111

112

Claude Debussy
(August 22, 1862 – March 25, 1918)

Debussy wanted to be a painter as a boy, but his father planned the life of a sailor for his son. A friend of the family, Maute de Fleurville, a pupil of Chopin, taught young Claude piano for three years, and at age 11 he entered the Paris Conservatoire. Debussy took instinctively to the so-called "organ-tuner's" scale, consisting of six whole tones. He was not an atonalist, but he opened the door for those who were to annihilate keys and key relationships.

Clair De Lune

Claude Debussy

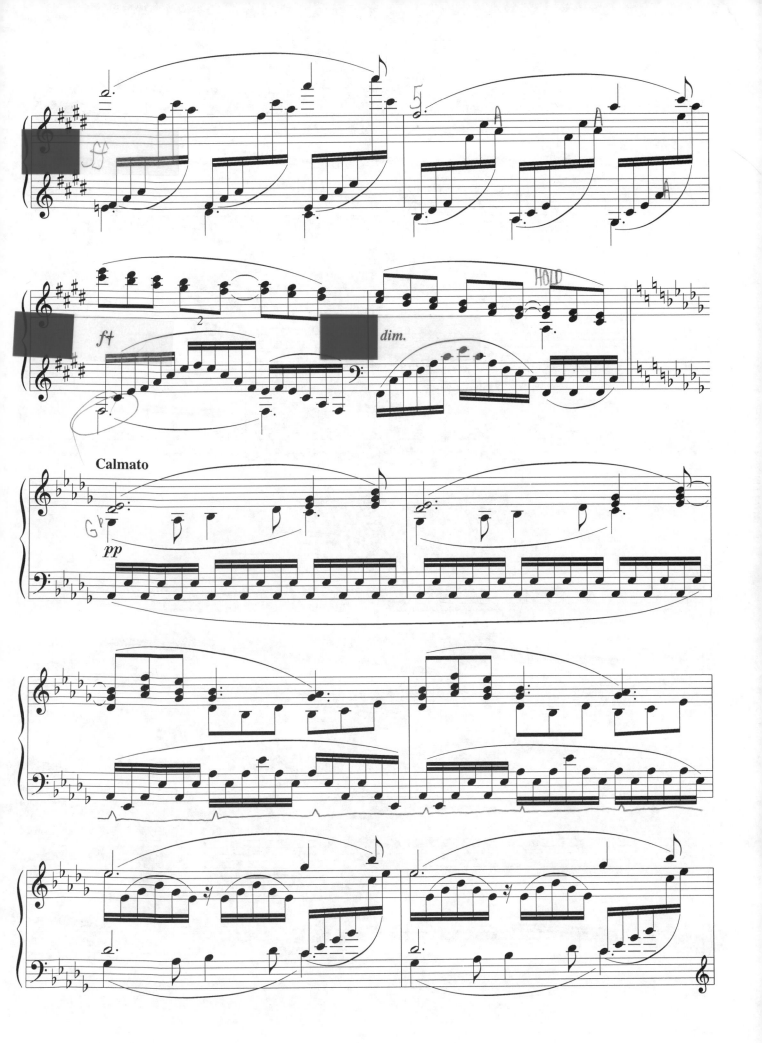

pp

don't speed

pp morendo jusquä la fin

OFF

Emaj

119

Sergei Rachmaninoff
(April 1, 1873 – March 28, 1943)

Rachmaninoff's father was the captain of the Imperial Guards, and he was born on an estate in Oneg. By the time Rachmaninoff was 10 years old, his father had lost a large part of the family fortune and his parents separated. He lived with his mother and he was spared going into military service. His mother encouraged his musical study, her father having been a pupil of John Field. Rachmaninoff studied composition with Arensky at the conservatory, but his idol was Tchaikovsky.

When Rachmaninoff was 20, he composed the C♯ minor prelude which made its way around the world with almost fantastic speed, carrying with it the name of the composer.

Prelude in C♯ minor
(Op. 3, No. 2)

Sergei Rachmaninoff

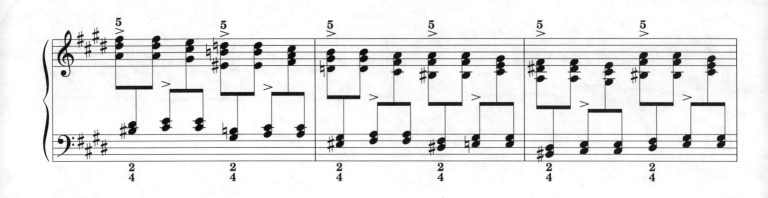

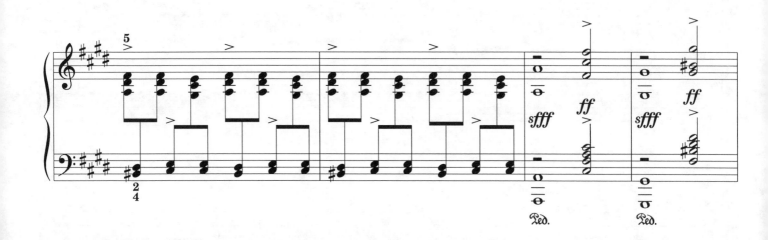

Tempo I

124

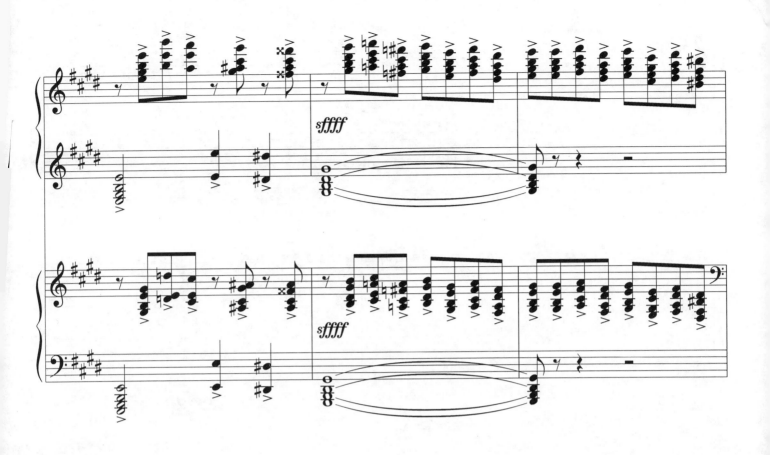

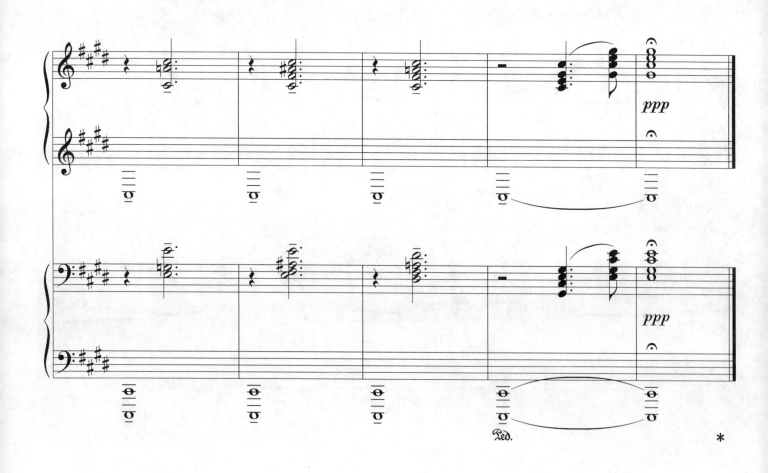

Prelude in G minor
(Op. 23, No. 5)

Sergei Rachmaninoff

Un poco meno mosso

dim. e rit.

ppp

poco a poco accelerando e cresc. al Tempo I

Tempo I

f

cresc.

132

133